JULIETTE GORDON *Low*

SPIRIT
of America®

JULIETTE GORDON *Low*

FOUNDER OF THE GIRL SCOUTS OF AMERICA

By Deborah Kent

Content Adviser: Katherine Knapp Keena, Program Manager,
Juliette Gordon Low Birthplace, Savannah, Georgia

The Child's World®
Chanhassen, Minnesota

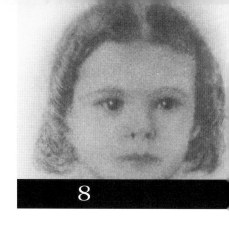

8

JULIETTE GORDON *Low*

Published in the United States of America by The Child's World®
PO Box 326 • Chanhassen, MN 55317-0326 • 800-599-READ • www.childsworld.com

Acknowledgments
The Child's World®: Mary Berendes, Publishing Director

Editorial Directions, Inc.: E. Russell Primm, Editorial Director; Pam Rosenberg, Line Editor; Elizabeth K. Martin, Assistant Editor; Olivia Nellums, Editorial Assistant; Susan Hindman, Copy Editor; Susan Ashley, Halley Gatenby, Proofreader; Jean Cotterell, Kevin Cunningham, Peter Garnham, Fact Checkers; Tim Griffin/IndexServ, Indexer; Dawn Friedman, Photo Researcher; Linda S. Koutris, Photo Selector

Photo
Cover: AP/Wide World Photos; AP/Wide World Photos: 2, 28; Bettmann/Corbis: 10, 24, 26; Corbis: 11; Historical Picture Archive/Corbis: 13; Stapleton Collection/Corbis: 17 top; Hulton-Deutsch Collection/Corbis: 18, 20; James Marshall/Corbis: 23; Hulton Archive/Getty Images: 16, 17 bottom, 19; Collection of the Juliette Gordon Low Birthplace, Girl Scout National Center, Savannah, GA: 6, 7, 8, 9, 12, 14, 15, 21, 22, 27; Library of Congress: 25.

Library of Congress Cataloging-in-Publication Data
Kent, Deborah.
  Juliette Gordon Low : founder of the Girl Scouts of America / by Deborah Kent.
    p. cm. — (Our people)
"Spirit of America."
Summary: Provides a brief introduction to Juliette Gordon Low, her accomplishments, and her impact on American history.
Includes bibliographical references and index.
  ISBN 1-59296-006-5 (lib. bdg. : alk. paper)
  1. Low, Juliette Gordon, 1860–1927—Juvenile literature. 2. Girl Scouts of the United States of America—Biography—Juvenile literature. 3. Girl Scouts—United States—Biography—Juvenile literature. [1. Low, Juliette Gordon, 1860–1927. 2. Girl Scouts of the United States of America—Biography. 3. Women—Biography.] I. Title. II. Series.
  HS3268.2.L68K45 2004
  369.463'092—dc21   2003004180

Contents

Chapter ONE

Daisy

EVERY YEAR, THOUSANDS OF GIRLS VISIT A LOVELY old house in Savannah, Georgia. The girls belong to a nationwide organization called the Girl Scouts of the United States of America. They travel from all parts of the country to see the birthplace of the remarkable woman who founded the Girl Scouts, Juliette Gordon Low.

Juliette Gordon was born in Savannah on October 31, 1860. When she was only a few months old, the United States was ripped apart by the terrible Civil War. Eleven Southern states **seceded,** or broke away, from the Union and formed a government of

Juliette Gordon Low was born in this home in Savannah, Georgia.

their own. They called themselves the Confederate States of America. This happened because leaders in those states disagreed with leaders in the North about slavery and other issues. Captain William Gordon, Juliette's father, left

Eleanor Kinzie Gordon and William W. Gordon II were Juliette Low's parents.

home to fight on the side of the South. Juliette's mother, Eleanor (Nellie) Kinzie Gordon, had grown up in Chicago, Illinois. She didn't believe in the Southern cause, but she was loyal to her husband.

During the war years, food and fuel were scarce in Savannah. The Gordons lived through many cold, hungry days. After the Union army invaded Georgia, the families of Confederate officers were ordered to evacuate Savannah. Nellie Gordon took her children to Chicago. In 1865, the South was defeated and the war came to an end.

Interesting Fact

▶ When Union general William T. Sherman invaded Georgia during the Civil War, Nellie Kinzie Gordon, Juliette's mother, entertained him in her home.

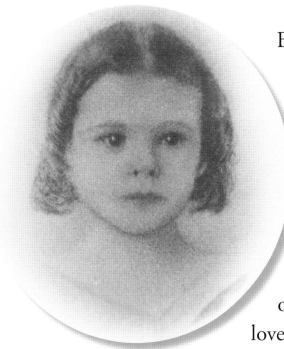

Daisy Gordon was four years old when this picture was taken.

Back in Savannah, the Gordon family was joyfully reunited. Juliette was the second in a family of six children. She loved to climb trees, ride horses, and make up stories of adventure. Creating art-works—sketches, paintings, and sculptures—was another one of her passions. She also loved animals. When she was born, her uncle in Chicago said that even though she was small and cried a lot, she would grow up to be a daisy. Family and friends called her Daisy for the rest of her life.

When Daisy was 13, her parents sent her away to the Virginia Female Institute, a boarding school in Virginia that is now called Stuart Hall. Girls at the school studied literature, music, drawing, composition, and a variety of other subjects. They also learned how to behave like proper young ladies. They were taught to walk gracefully, to curtsy, and to make polite conversation. For Daisy, who loved to run, climb, and play rough games, becoming a lady was a real struggle.

8

Though Daisy loved her friends at school, she couldn't wait for summer vacations. One summer, she got to know a family of Italian **immigrants** who sold fruits and vegetables on Savannah's streets. The family was poor and the children wore ragged hand-me-downs. Daisy organized a group of friends and cousins to sew the children some new clothes. She named her sewing club the Helping Hands.

Daisy was 10 years old when this picture was taken.

Unfortunately, Daisy had no idea how to teach sewing to them. She barely knew how to thread a needle. However, the group managed to make some clothes and gave them to the poor children. One day, the children got into a fight while wearing their new clothes. The clothing fell apart, and the children ran home with nothing on! After that, Daisy's brother renamed the club the Helpless Hands.

After four years at the Virginia Female Institute,

Daisy followed her older sister to another boarding school in Virginia called Edge Hill. Then she went on to Mademoiselle Charbonnier's, a **finishing school** in New York City. She continued with her art studies and learned to speak **fluent** French. By the time she graduated from Charbonnier's, Daisy was a lovely young woman, ready to take her place in Savannah society.

Daisy was a popular young woman who attended many parties and dances.

At that time, most educated southern girls were not expected to find jobs and support themselves. It would have been normal for Daisy to turn her attention to finding a husband, settling down, and starting a family. She went to lots of dances, parties, carriage rides, and picnics. She met many young men who were looking for a young woman to marry. Daisy received several marriage proposals, but she turned them down. She liked the young men she knew in Savannah. Yet none of them inspired her to fall in love.

THE AMERICAN CIVIL WAR BEGAN ON APRIL 12, 1861. ON THAT DAY, THE Confederate army fired on Fort Sumter (below) in Charleston, South Carolina. The tensions between the North and South had been building for a long time. The economy of the South was mainly agricultural. Most of the farms were large plantations, which required slave labor to make them profitable. In the North, manufacturing was becoming a bigger part of the economy. Farms there were smaller, and farmers did not use slave labor. Most people in the North did not want slavery to be legal in the western territories of the United States. The Southern states did not want any restrictions on slavery in the territories. They feared that if slavery was not allowed in new states formed out of the western territories, eventually slavery would be made illegal throughout the whole country.

The election of Abraham Lincoln to the presidency in 1860 proved to be the breaking point. Lincoln was opposed to expanding slavery into the western territories but was willing to allow slavery to continue in the Southern states. This was not enough to keep the country together. Soon after his election, South Carolina seceded from the Union, followed by ten more Southern states.

Like many families, the Gordons were torn by divided loyalties during the Civil War. Juliette Gordon's father fought for the South. Her mother's father, two brothers, and uncles fought for the North. Juliette Gordon Low was proud of her Northern ancestors, but she thought of herself as a Southerner all her life.

Chapter TWO

An English Lady

Daisy Gordon (standing, third from left) and Willy Low (seated, third from left) with a group of friends

BY THE TIME DAISY WAS 22, SHE SEEMED NO closer to marriage. In 1882, Mr. and Mrs. Gordon sent Daisy on a long trip to Europe. In France, Italy, and Great Britain, she saw the sights and mingled with high society. In England, Daisy met a dashing young man named William Mackay Low. Willy's good looks and his cheerful, fun-loving spirit enchanted her. Surely she had found the man of her dreams.

Willy Low's father was a very

wealthy shipping **magnate** with homes and business interests in Savannah and England. Willy was used to a life of comfort and pleasure, with never a thought of work. Compared to the

This picture of Regents Circus in London, England, shows what the city was like at the time Daisy was traveling in Europe.

Lows, the Gordons lived a very **modest** lifestyle. Willy wanted to marry Daisy, but he was afraid that his father would disapprove. For months, he insisted on keeping their courtship a secret. Daisy also wanted to keep the courtship secret because she knew her father would not approve of Willy.

In 1884, Daisy made a second trip to England. Her parents realized that she was in love with Willy Low. Her father grew concerned. In a letter he told her, "An honest man who has learned to work and support himself is preferable to a man born rich." Willy had no direction in life. Could he really make Daisy happy?

The more their parents objected, the more strongly Daisy and Willy believed they

Juliette Gordon and Willy Low were married on December 21, 1886.

had found true love. At last, both families **relented.** The Gordons prepared for a splendid wedding to be held in Savannah.

Daisy threw herself into the excitement of choosing bridesmaids' dresses, planning menus, and being fitted for her bridal gown. Several months before the wedding, she developed a painful ear infection. This was not unusual because she had a history of ear problems. But this time, despite treatment, the infection grew steadily worse. Eventually, she lost most of the hearing in her left ear.

Daisy Gordon and Willy Low were married in Savannah on December 21, 1886. On their wedding day, well-wishers pelted them with handfuls of rice. A grain of rice lodged in Daisy's right ear. As a result, she lost hearing in her right ear, too. For the rest of her life, she was almost completely deaf.

The Lows owned or rented homes in England, Scotland, and Savannah. They

14

divided their time among all three places. They enjoyed hosting lavish parties for their rich friends. One of Willy's friends was Britain's Prince of Wales, who later became King Edward VII. Daisy Low was formally presented to the king and queen at the Royal Court.

Daisy's deafness made it difficult for her to follow conversation at parties. Though she couldn't listen easily to others, she captured their attention by telling stories. Some of her stories described funny things that happened to her on her travels. Others told of her ancestors and their adventures as pioneers in Illinois. Daisy's stories drew people to her and won her countless admirers.

Willy loved to go hunting. As the years passed, he spent more and more time on long hunting trips in Africa, India, and other far-flung places. While he was away, Daisy missed him terribly. Her talent for art was a great comfort to her. She filled her lonely days with drawing and sculpting. She even learned the craft of metalwork and

Juliette Low made this sculpture of her father. He is wearing the uniform of a general in the U.S. Volunteer Army during the Spanish-American War (1898).

designed a set of **ornate** gates for the Low house in Warwickshire, England.

Daisy seemed to have everything a woman could desire. She was wealthy and beautiful. Her friends adored her. Beneath the surface, however, lurked a deep sadness. Her husband often drank heavily. When he was drunk, he said cruel things to Daisy. He also had relationships with other women. Willy died in 1905 from illnesses related to his **alcoholism** and lifestyle.

Sir Robert Baden-Powell was a friend of Juliette Gordon Low.

Daisy had loved her husband despite their unhappy marriage. She began to wonder what she could do with the rest of her life. "I am just an **idle** woman of the world," she wrote to her mother, "with no real work or duties. I would like to get away from the world somewhere and work at sculpting—start to do some work in life." But not even her artwork provided the sense of purpose Daisy needed. She continued to search and discovered that purpose at last through a remarkable new friend, Sir Robert Baden-Powell.

16

PRINCE OF WALES IS AN honorary title given to the male heir to the British throne. In general, the heir is the oldest son of the reigning king or queen. The title Prince of Wales dates back to 1301, when England's King Edward I gave it to his son.

Edward VII was born on November 9, 1841. As the oldest son of Queen Victoria, he held the title Prince of Wales until he took the throne. He became King Edward VII upon the death of his mother in 1901. As a young man, he rebelled against his mother by living a life of excess. He drank, gambled, and had relationships with women other than his wife. Despite all of this, Edward VII was popular with the British people. He was an excellent diplomat and became known as Edward the Peacemaker. He died on May 6, 1910.

Chapter THREE

"Something for the Girls"

Two Boy Scouts pose holding flagpoles

DAISY LOW MET SIR ROBERT BADEN-POWELL at a luncheon in London in 1911. He had started a new organization to teach tracking, signaling, and other outdoor skills to boys in Great Britain. The organization was called the Boy Scouts.

When the Boy Scouts had its first rally, 6,000 girls signed up using their first initials and last names. The girls wanted to be Scouts, too. Baden-Powell got his sister Agnes to start organizing the girls in a sister group called the Girl Guides. He told Low that thousands of girls wanted to join. She was fascinated. Perhaps the Girl Guides could use her help.

In 1911, Low started her first Girl Guide group, or patrol, at her home in the Scottish countryside.

Some of the first members of the Girl Guides worked together to build their own headquarters.

Seven girls from nearby farms attended her meetings on Saturday afternoons. Low always served tea with delicious cakes and sandwiches. The girls came from poor families and were delighted to taste such dainty treats.

Low planned interesting activities for every meeting. She taught the girls first aid, cooking, and knot-tying. Soon she was searching for long-term projects. Often children from the area were sent to work in factories in the cities. Low looked for ways her girls could earn money right at home. She and the Girl Guides raised chickens and

Interesting Fact

▶ Juliette Gordon Low's birthplace became a registered National Historic Landmark in 1965.

19

sold the eggs. Another project was spinning. The Girl Guides learned to card, or clean, raw wool as it came from the sheep. Then they spun it into woolen yarn that brought a fine price.

The Girl Guide movement spread quickly throughout Great Britain. After she started more companies of Girl Guides in London, Low was convinced that girls in the United States would like to become Girl Guides, too. As she set out on her next visit to Georgia, her mind whirled with plans for starting Girl Guide patrols in the United States. On her first night in Savannah, Low phoned her cousin, Nina Anderson Pape, the headmistress of a school for girls.

Girl Guides from London raise their flag while at a camp in France.

"Come right over," Low insisted. "I've got something for the girls of Savannah, and all of America, and all the world, and we're going to start it tonight!"

20

As soon as Low described the Girl Guide program, Pape wanted to help. She knew several girls who belonged to a nature club. They went for hikes in the woods, studying trees, flowers, and birds. Surely these girls would be thrilled to become Girl Guides. As Pape recruited girls, Low gathered the support of her influential Savannah friends and relatives. By the time the Girl Guides held its first meeting, Daisy Low had persuaded her mother and ten other Savannah ladies to serve as the first Board of Councilors.

Nina Anderson Pape (far left) and a group of Girl Scout leaders.

Juliette Gordon Low and a group of Girl Scouts posed for this picture in 1924. It was taken in Savannah, Georgia, at the spot where the organization was founded.

On March 12, 1912, 18 girls in two patrols were registered as the first official Girl Guides of the United States of America. (Low changed the name from Girl Guides to Girl Scouts in 1913.) To this day, Girl Scouts in the United States celebrate March 12 as the birthday of their movement.

TODAY, SOME 2.8 MILLION GIRLS IN THE UNITED STATES BELONG TO THE GIRL Scouts. About 8.5 million girls in 140 countries are involved in Girl Scout and Girl Guide programs. Any girl between the ages of 5 and 17 who accepts the Girl Scouts' promise and law is **eligible** to join. Girl Scouts advance through five levels based on age, from Daisy Girl Scouts (ages 5 through 7) to Senior Girl Scouts (14 to 17). The Daisy Girl Scouts are named after the founder, Juliette "Daisy" Low.

The Girl Scout program has four main goals. The organization is committed to helping its members develop to their full potential. It works to foster relationship skills and help girls develop a strong set of personal values. In addition, Girl Scouts are expected to use their skills for the benefit of their communities.

Girls Scouts work on projects in many areas. These include the arts, physical fitness, and math, science, and technology-related projects. Adult leaders encourage the girls to explore their interests and develop new skills. The skills and values that girls develop in the Girl Scout program serve them well throughout their lives.

Chapter FOUR

The Hundred-Horsepower Engine

Juliette Gordon Low traveled throughout the United States to bring the Girl Scout movement to as many girls as possible.

AS THE GIRL SCOUTS TOOK HOLD IN Savannah, Juliette Low worked to spread the movement throughout the United States. One of her friends wrote to her, "You must be the hundred-horsepower engine that drives the airplane." The Girl Scouts were the plane, driven by Low's tireless energy. She traveled the country, talking to leading businessmen and their wives. She spoke to the wives of congressmen and government officials. Her charm and enthusiasm won unfailing support. She asked Mrs. Woodrow Wilson, wife of the president of the United

States, to become the first honorary president of the Girl Scouts. Mrs. Wilson agreed, and since then every U.S. president's wife has served as honorary president. Low established a national office for the Girl Scouts in Washington, D.C. The headquarters later moved to New York.

Low's life was a whirl of activity. "I do not know how she lives it all," her mother wrote, "losing things every hour—telephoning every minute—changing her plans every second!" Once, Low sent a telegram to the Washington office, asking someone to meet her "in New York, Baltimore, Washington, or Boston."

Mrs. Woodrow Wilson was the first honorary president of the Girl Scouts of the United States.

During World War I, Girl Scouts worked on many projects to benefit the war effort.

You Save Peach Seeds — They Will Save Soldiers' Lives

When the United States entered World War I in 1917, the Girl Scouts threw themselves into the war effort. They sewed bandages for wounded soldiers. They planted vegetable gardens and sold war bonds. They also learned telegraphy to help the war effort. As president of the Girl Scouts of the United States, Low rushed from city to city, encouraging Scout troops and raising money for the movement. Wherever she went, she wore her Girl Scout uniform. A knife, a whistle, and a tin drinking cup hung from her belt.

Low returned to England when the war ended in 1918 and resumed her work with the British Girl Guides. By now, the movement had reached many other countries as well. The first International Council of Girl Guides and Girl Scouts met in London in 1919. Juliette Low represented the Girl Scouts of the United States of America.

In 1920, Low retired as president and took the title of founder. She continued to travel between England and the United States and spent much of her time building worldwide support for the Girl Scouts. When she was in the United States, she attended Girl Scout troop meetings and joined the girls on hikes and camping trips. She loved to sit with

Juliette Gordon Low (standing, fourth from left) with a group of Girl Scouts at the first Girl Scout Headquarters

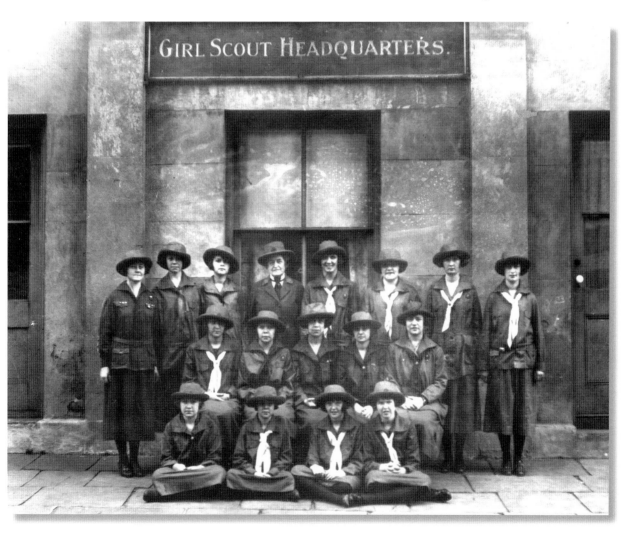

them around a crackling campfire, telling ghost stories and tales of her pioneer ancestors. Low never had children of her own. The Girl Scouts provided her with an ever-growing family of children all over the world.

After a four-year battle with breast cancer, Juliette Low died in Savannah on January 17, 1927. As she requested, she was buried in her Girl Scout uniform. In the breast pocket was a telegram from the president of the Girl Scouts of the United States. The telegram read, "You are not only the first Girl Scout but the best Girl Scout of them all."

1860   Juliette Gordon is born on October 31 in Savannah, Georgia.

1861   The Civil War begins just months after Juliette Gordon is born.

1865   The Civil War ends in April when the South surrenders.

1873   Gordon enters the Virginia Female Institute, a boarding school.

1882   On her first trip to Europe, Gordon meets her future husband, William Mackay Low.

1886   Juliette Gordon and William Low are married.

1905   William Low dies.

1911   Juliette Low meets Sir Robert Baden-Powell and becomes interested in the British Girl Guide movement.

1912   On March 12 in Savannah, Low holds the first Girl Scouts meeting in the United States.

1917   The United States enters World War I. Girl Scouts begin working on projects to help the war effort.

1918   Low returns to England and resumes her work with the British Girl Guides.

1919   The first International Council of Girl Guides and Girl Scouts meets in London; Low represents the United States.

1920   Low retires as president of the Girl Scouts of the United States of America and takes the title of founder.

1927   On January 17, Low dies in Savannah.

1965   Juliette Gordon Low's birthplace becomes a National Historic Landmark.

1979   Juliette Gordon Low is inducted into the Women's Hall of Fame

Glossary TERMS

alcoholism (AL-kuh-hol-izm)
Alcoholism is a disease in which a person becomes addicted to the alcohol found in drinks such as wine and beer. Juliette Low's husband died because of his alcoholism.

eligible (EL-uh-juh-buhl)
If you are eligible for something, you have the right qualifications. Any girl between the ages of five and seventeen is eligible to join the Girl Scouts.

finishing school (FIN-ish-ing SKOOL)
A finishing school is a school for young women that teaches the skills necessary for a successful entry into adult life in upper-class society. Juliette Gordon Low attended Mademoiselle Charbonnier's finishing school in New York City.

fluent (FLOO-uhnt)
To be fluent in a language means to speak it smoothly and flawlessly. Juliette Low was fluent in French.

idle (EYE-duhl)
Idle means unoccupied, having nothing to do. Before she started the Girl Scouts, Juliette Low thought of herself as an idle woman.

immigrants (IM-uh-gruhnts)
Immigrants are people who leave their homeland and move to a new country. Juliette Low wanted to make clothes for some immigrant children in Savannah.

magnate (MAG-nate)
A magnate is a person who has great power or influence in a specific area. Juliette Low's father-in-law was a shipping magnate.

modest (MOD-ist)
Modest means simple or not extreme. Compared to the Lows, the Gordons lived a modest lifestyle.

ornate (or-NAYT)
Ornate means fancy and decorated. Juliette Low designed the ornate gates for her house in Warwickshire.

relented (ri-LENT-ed)
When you say someone relented, you mean that they gave in or became less strict. Daisy's parents disapproved of her marriage to Willy, but finally they relented.

seceded (si-SEED-ed)
A group that has seceded has broken away from a larger group or organization, usually to form its own organization. The Civil War began when eleven Southern states seceded from the Union and formed the Confederate States of America.

For Further INFORMATION

Web Sites

Visit our homepage for lots of links about Juliette Gordon Low:
http://www.childsworld.com/links.html

Note to Parents, Teachers, and Librarians:
We routinely verify our Web links to make sure they're safe,
active sites—so encourage your readers to check them out!

Books

Brown, Fern. *Daisy and the Girl Scouts: The Story of Juliette Gordon Low.* Morton Grove, Ill.: Albert Whitman, 1996.

Higgins, Helen Boyd, and Cathy Morrison (illustrator). *Juliette Low: Girl Scout Founder.* Carmel, Ind.: Patria Press, 2002.

Pace, Mildred Mastin. *Juliette Low.* Ashland, Ky.: The Jesse Stuart Foundation, 1997.

Places to Visit or Contact

Juliette Gordon Low Birthplace
To visit the home where Juliette Gordon Low was born, which has been restored to look much as it did in 1886, the year she was married
10 East Oglethorpe Avenue
Savannah, GA 31401
912/233-4501

Girl Scouts of the U.S.A.
To get more information about the Girl Scouts
420 Fifth Avenue
New York, NY 10018-2798
800/478-7248

Index

About the Author

DEBORAH KENT GREW UP IN LITTLE FALLS, NEW JERSEY, AND received her bachelor's degree from Oberlin College. She earned a master's degree from Smith College School for Social Work and worked as a social worker before becoming a full-time writer. She is the author of 18 young-adult novels and more than 50 nonfiction titles for children. She lives in Chicago with her husband, children's author R. Conrad Stein, and their daughter, Janna.